FOUNDATIONS MANUAL

The Prosperous Soul©

STEWARDSHIP SERIES

By Stephen De Silva

Published by

Accent Digital Publishing, Inc
2932 Churn Creek Rd
Redding , CA 96002

Accentdigitalpublishing.com

ISBN 978-60445-019-4

Graphic Design by Linda Lee

Acknowledgements

"Friendship is like a prism through which the many variations of beauty are revealed in our lives."

Anon.

Dawna, Cory, and Tim—for you, I would fight a bear, and win.

Pam, Carol, Raina and Linda—I could not have done this without you.

CONTENTS

INTRODUCTION

<u>3 John 1:2</u> "Beloved, I pray that in all respects you may prosper and be in good health, just as your soul prospers."

SESSION OVERVIEW

WHY ARE WE HERE?

I designed this class with two goals in mind. The first goal is to recover the meaning of the biblical term, "prosperous soul."[1] The term is pregnant with meaning but too often carelessly tossed about in conversation. Overused, the term becomes familiar and commonplace. My first goal is to "re-open" the deep well of meaning and drink deeply of this vital biblical truth.

The second goal of this class is breakthrough. For those who suffer under a poverty spirit, I seek the destruction of that evil stronghold. For those who already walk in freedom, I seek promotion, advancement, and increase. Idle talk about the concepts of a poverty spirit and a prosperous soul hold no interest for me; the Bible warns us away from mere speculation. My second goal is, simply put, the invasion of a supernatural heaven into a natural world. "On earth as it is in heaven."[2] If this class enables you to begin or advance your own prosperity of soul, then we both have succeeded.

Each time I teach this material, I learn a little bit more about a prosperous soul. It has become the journey of my life. Thankfully, God promises to reveal His secrets to us if we are willing to search out a matter. And that is what we will do in this class. We will prospect the clear river of God's Word for the treasures He has hidden for us.

In the book of Genesis, Joseph's life displayed a remarkable example of success.[3] Joseph served as a great model of stewardship, handling well the responsibilities of power and favor and position. Joseph succeeded in his calling with strength of character. We, too, are called to stewardship. We are called to strength of character. Only a prosperous soul can successfully carry the assignment of power and favor and position. Success, defined as fulfilling God's assignment, is what a prosperous soul is for. I believe success is God's idea.

This class is always changing, thriving on new situations and revelations. To me, this vigorous process is evidence of God's supernatural involvement in a topic that many people consider to be dry and static. I tell my students that this is not a class about money. Rather, this is a class about wealth. Most studies on money rely on formula and training: brute force regimen. Surely persistence, discipline, and self-control are vital elements of a prosperous soul. But those elements must cooperate with others like inspiration, revelation, and vision. I see more for the steward than columns of numbers. I see cities where once were minas.[4]

The apostle Paul prayed that we would be filled with "all spiritual wisdom."[5] This manual is designed to draw on this prayer, which is part of our rich heritage as followers of Christ. It is not enough to merely observe wisdom. We are here to apprehend the wisdom Paul prayed and to truly embrace that wisdom, making it our own.

I am familiar with the spirit of poverty. I have not struggled like so many people in third-world countries. I have not suffered under heavy-handed governments in war-torn corners of the world. Instead, I lived much of my early life under the influence of a poverty mentality. Thankfully, God addressed this lifestyle at the cross.

I have heard it said that fear is the expectation of evil. This is a true statement. I am replacing, brick by brick, my expectation of evil with an expectation of good. I have discovered a key in the destruction of a spirit of poverty and the reconstruction of a prosperous soul. I look forward to sharing these secrets with you, the secrets of *A Prosperous Soul.*

SESSION ONE

DREAMING IN GOD

Gen. 37:19 "They said to one another, 'Here comes this dreamer!'"

SESSION OVERVIEW

Considering Your Heart

Blaming the Dreamer

Dream Exercise

Afraid to Dream

Dreaming in God

Sozo Prayer

CONSIDERING YOUR HEART

Find yourself somewhere between the two extremes of prosperity and poverty. Mark your place.

PROSPERITY ——————————————— POVERTY

Next, draw an arrow from your mark in the direction of prosperity. Be sure to draw your line past the end, into the margin and off the page. This is a graphic picture of doing "far more abundantly beyond all that we ask or think…" Look at your arrow. This was a prophetic act. What lies off the margin for you?

BLAMING THE DREAMER

Consider the man, Joseph. His life of divine purpose and purity is nothing short of miraculous. Joseph was the beloved son of his parents, Jacob and Rachael. Joseph was kidnapped, enslaved, entitled, imprisoned, forgotten, remembered, admired, empowered, and vindicated. But through all of these ups and downs, Joseph was always a dreamer. This is no accident.

Consider the timeline of Joseph's life, beginning with his first recorded dream concerning his father and brothers. His proclamation was not well received by his kin. In fact, it was so unacceptable in his culture for the younger to speak of subjugation of his elders that his dream and interpretation were flatly rejected. Even Joseph's father responded with a rebuke:

> *Gen. 37:9-11* *"Now he had still another dream, and related it to his brothers, and said, 'Lo, I have had still another dream; and behold, the sun and the moon and eleven stars were bowing down to me.' He related it to his father and to his brothers; and his father rebuked him and said to him, 'What is this dream that you have had? Shall I and your mother and your brothers actually come to bow ourselves down before you to the ground?' His brothers were jealous of him, but his father kept the saying in mind."*

Joseph's dream affected the rest of his life, but not in the way we may think. We may think that Joseph suffered because of his dream. Instead, consider that the attack on Joseph flowed out of his brothers' poverty spirit. In fact, all of Joseph's suffering and trials were the result of the exposure of the poverty in others because of Joseph's light. Joseph was not a victim of his dreaming. It was the dream that illuminated Joseph's prosperous soul, and uncovered the poverty in those around him. It was God's favor (in the form of a dream) that buoyed Joseph to the top time and time again.

In spite of the low places he passed through, Joseph was faithful to dream; Joseph was faithful in every turn and time. His faithfulness and integrity gave Joseph the capacity to carry the dream to completion. It is remarkable to see that the dream produced its favorable fruit at every recorded phase of his life, phases of exaltation and humiliation.

In captivity, Joseph succeeded:

> *Gen. 39:2-3 "The LORD was with Joseph, so he became a successful man. And he was in the house of his master, the Egyptian. Now his master saw that the LORD was with him and how the LORD caused all that he did to prosper in his hand."*

In jail, Joseph succeeded again:

> *Gen. 39:21-22 "But the LORD was with Joseph and extended kindness to him, and gave him favor in the sight of the chief jailer. The chief jailer committed to Joseph's charge all the prisoners who were in the jail; so that whatever was done there, he was responsible for it."*

Finally, in Pharaoh's court, Joseph succeeded once again:

> *Gen. 41:40-41* *"'You shall be over my house, and according to your command all my people shall do homage; only in the throne I will be greater than you.' Pharaoh said to Joseph, 'See, I have set you over all the land of Egypt.'"*

I consider Joseph's lifestyle of dreaming to be one of the vital keys to a prosperous soul. According to scripture, abundance is part of the life that Christ prescribed:

> *John 10:10* *"The thief comes only to steal and kill and destroy; I came that they may have life, and have it abundantly."*

The dream is vital. Begin to feed your dream once again.

DREAM EXERCISE

Take five minutes to complete these questions. Stir your faith and dream high. You have permission to "go big." Consider this verse:

> *Eph. 3:20* *"Now to Him who is able to do far more abundantly beyond all that we ask or think, according to the power that works within us…"*

One dream I will fulfill will be to

_____

_____

_____

_____

Twenty years from now, I will

_____

_____

_____

_____

I imagine that I can

_____

_____

_____

_____

AFRAID TO DREAM

Some of us have suffered loss or disappointment to the point of being afraid to dream. Rather than risk more disappointment, we hide or occupy ourselves to the point of excess. We protect ourselves with lack. Poverty becomes a shell.

Some hardships are thrust upon us and some are self-inflicted. Regardless of the cause, we can lose our capacity to dream.

> _Proverbs 13:12_ "Hope deferred makes the heart sick, but desire fulfilled is a tree of life."

> _Psalms 71:14_ "But as for me, I will hope continually, and will praise You yet more and more."

> _Proverbs 23:18_ "Surely there is a future, and your hope will not be cut off."

> _Proverbs 24:14_ "Know that wisdom is thus for your soul; If you find it, then there will be a future, and your hope will not be cut off."

Without hope, we run the risk of living a deferred life, merely existing day-to-day and sick of heart. This is a condition of dis-ease (disease). We cannot tolerate hopelessness in the body of Christ.

Living in hope invites the dream. It is a life lived forward in expectation and anticipation. It is life more abundant. I call it _up-living_.

DREAMING IN GOD

Consider Jesus' prescription for hope. Digest these rich truths slowly. Meditate on them until your heart is softened by scripture.

John 15:7 "If you abide in Me, and My words abide in you, ask whatever you wish, and it will be done for you."

John 15:16 "You did not choose Me but I chose you, and appointed you that you would go and bear fruit, and that your fruit would remain, so that whatever you ask of the Father in My name He may give to you."

John 14:14 "If you ask Me anything in My name, I will do it."

John 16:23-24 "In that day you will not question Me about anything. Truly, truly, I say to you, if you ask the Father for anything in My name, He will give it to you. Until now you have asked for nothing in My name; ask and you will receive, so that your joy may be made full."

SOZO[1] PRAYER

Begin with worship. Pray and ask Father God to show Himself to you. Wait for the sense of safety in His presence, perhaps sitting in His lap or resting beside Him. Linger with this exercise until you see or sense His loving presence, His great protection. Meditate on His greatness and care for your wellbeing.[2] Don't be in a hurry. Describe how being in God's presence makes you feel.

In Father God's presence, I experience _____
_____
_____
_____
_____
_____

From this safe place, ask Him to reopen your ability to dream. Ask for His help in re-digging the well of sanctified dreams and imaginations in your life. If you discover feelings of fear or hopelessness, ask the Holy Spirit to show you the events that damaged your ability to dream. Wait for Him to show you a picture of where or when these feelings began. This picture usually comes quickly and surprisingly easily, so relax and listen. When you see the picture, write a simple description of what God showed you.

In my mind, I saw pictured _____

_____

_____

_____

Reflecting on the picture, ask God this question: What lie did I learn when that event happened to me? Listen for His reply; the answer may not be what you expect, so be patient. In as few words as possible, write a simple label for the lie you learned.

The lie I learned was _____

_____

_____

_____

Ask God if your label is correct. Allow Him to change it or distill the label further if He so chooses. Consider what God revealed and examine the original event again. Ask the Father what the truth really was. Again, listen for His wise answer. In as few words as possible, write a simple description of the truth to replace that lie.

God showed me the truth of that event: _____

_____

_____

_____

_____

_____

At this point, you are still resting in safety with God. You are looking back at the event with Father God's help. As a born-again believer in Jesus Christ, you are a new creature, loved and accepted. From this place of protection, forgive and release every person you saw, one by one, with God's help. Ask God to forgive them as well. Remember, you will experience freedom only to the extent that you forgive others.[2] Do not leave this place until you sense your release. Having forgiven everyone who God brings to your memory, now you are ready for a declaration. Repeat this aloud several times:

"I, _____(say your name), declare my emancipation (freedom) from pain, fear, bitterness, and disappointments. I declare my liberty to live in prosperity. I am a child of God. I am a blessed man/woman and God favors me. He is inviting me to live a life of dreams and I choose to receive this gift now."

Place your hand on your heart and prophesy to yourself the following prayer:

"Jesus, I am your beloved and You are mine. I am being perfected by You, the author and finisher of faith. You have great plans for me, beyond what I can ask or think, and I cooperate with You. So, I REOPEN my dreams and visions. I RELIGHT my hope. I RELEASE my redeemed imagination."

Linger in this moment. Do not leave this place of prayer until you sense God's presence and grace for you to dream again.

So much of what a person believes to be true becomes true for that person. As people, we have a powerful need to build our understanding of truth around our events and experiences. This need is not evil; it enables society and creates the fabric of our culture, even our identity. However, the conclusions we reach as individuals are like seeds that we sow throughout our lives. If we reach wrong conclusions, we will harvest the bad fruit of those bad beliefs. We will discuss this much more in session 3, but for now we can celebrate God's mercy and grace, handed to us for a successful life. Let's move forward together and see what other treasures He has in store. Capture this moment by completing Appendix 1.

Touch your head and say, "I am a prosperous soul."

SESSION TWO

STEWARDSHIP

<u>Heb. 11:6</u> *"And without faith it is impossible to please Him, for he who comes to God must believe that He is and that He is a rewarder of those who seek Him."*

SESSION OVERVIEW

Up-Living

The Black Swan

Power of the Testimony

Whatever You Ask

Stewardship

Hermit Crab Prophecies

The Wealth of Nations

UP-LIVING

Throughout scripture we see God with us.[1] He is naturally supernatural. We are told in the gospel of John that we would do greater things than these.[2] What did Jesus mean by that statement?

Will we heal the sick and cast out demons? Will we live in divine health? Are these scriptures for us today? The answer is an emphatic "yes." We are to do miracles, signs, and wonders. We are to base our actions upon God's Word, the absolute truth.

Many of us have had powerful experiences in our lives, some good and some bad. The ones we embrace will define our perception of reality.

Our mind builds a "map" of what is true and discards as false what we don't understand. When we do this, truth only forms around our understanding and we become the highest authority on what is true. Simply put, this is arrogance of the highest order.

Consider the idea of praying for the sick. Some great teachers have built entire doctrines to argue why miracles are not for today. Since they have not seen a healing or miracle, they conclude that God does not heal today. Others begin bravely enough, but falter when their prayers and hopes do not seem to produce results. Pain, suffering, and death shout so loudly that the soft voice of hope is drowned out.

Some prayers appear unanswered, yet the Word of God is clear. The Bible sets the bar far above our experience, and asks us to live by faith at that high level. In spite of what we experience, we are to live with the expectation of miracles and signs and wonders. God invites us into up-living in His invisible Kingdom.

THE BLACK SWAN

Forming an internalized map of reality is a necessary part of being human. This mapping is a valuable tool that enables us to relate in our world and remain sane. But like most things in life, overusing any tool can become a detriment. We are not the highest authority on what is true. What we don't know can hurt us.

A recent author brilliantly describes this aspect of human nature. I quote:

> "Before the discovery of Australia, people in the Old World were convinced that all swans were white, an unassailable belief as it seemed completely confirmed by empirical evidence. The sighting of the first Black Swan might have been an interesting surprise for a few ornithologists, but that is not where the significance of the story lies. It illustrates a severe limitation to our learning from observations or experience and the fragility of our knowledge. One single observation can invalidate a general statement derived from millennia of confirmatory sightings of millions of white swans. All you need is one single (and, I am told, quite ugly) black bird."[3]

So, what happens to our mental map when we see a genuine miracle? What happens when we hear or read testimonies of supernatural happenings?

The miracle, the sign, and the wonder are Black Swans. These events cast new light on our perception of reality. They shift our paradigm of what is real. They invite us further than our experience would take us. Believers in Jesus Christ have chosen a lifestyle of unlimited potential, a lifestyle of Black Swans.

Because of that potential, we carry an explosive possibility into every aspect of our lives—as parents, as friends, as entrepreneurs…. We can choose to live differently and lean into the miraculous. We can expect to live with a prosperous soul.

THE POWER OF THE TESTIMONY

The power of the testimony is a fundamental core value of Bethel Church culture. We believe it is our privilege and responsibility to preserve the stories of God's activities in our lives. The testimony serves as a memorial to the divine events in our daily lives, our Black Swans. We listen for what God is doing around us. We catch a glimpse of God's giving nature each time we hear of a miraculous healing or a financial breakthrough. Each testimony becomes a celebration and a prophetic announcement of what Christ is doing through us and for us. These reports become invitations from God to join in for ourselves.

The apostle John referred to the testimony of Jesus as being the *very spirit* (emphasis added) of prophecy. I believe John is saying that sharing the things God has done for others is a prophetic declaration of what God will do for us.

> *Rev. 19:10b* *"worship God. For the testimony of Jesus is the spirit of prophecy."*[4]

I am continually hearing reports of financial breakthroughs, escapes and successes. Many times these answers are so significant and surprising that I think to myself, *O my gosh, I'll never forget that miracle.* And still, I find it is one of my biggest challenges to remember what has happened. I listen intently to a friend's successful journey through crisis and wonder how God pulled that off. I walk away inspired, but then forget to carry it in my heart like a new weapon. Part of the unique culture of Bethel Church is that we are a community which values the testimony and continually draws upon that from one another. The author of Hebrews tells us to live in this way:

> *Heb. 10:24-25* *"and let us consider how to stimulate one another to love and good deeds, not forsaking our own assembling together, as is the habit of some, but encouraging one another; and all the more as you see the day drawing near."*

Think of some Black Swan (miracles or breakthrough) testimonies of which you are aware. These can come from your own life or from the lives of others. List these in the spaces below: _____

_____

_____

_____

_____

How recent are these testimonies? Do you think God is actively doing things today? Is it possible you have overlooked some testimonies? What can you do to develop the skill of valuing the testimony in your daily life? List these in the spaces below:_____

_____

_____

_____

_____

WHATEVER YOU ASK

I have always squirmed at certain "absolute" statements in scripture. I squirm because it requires something from me beyond my experience and my comfort, perhaps even my doctrine. One of those statements is "Whatever you ask."

> _John 14:13_ *"Whatever you ask in My name, that will I do, so that the Father may be glorified in the Son."*

> _John 15:16_ *"You did not choose Me but I chose you, and appointed you that you would go and bear fruit, and that your fruit would remain, so that whatever you ask of the Father in My name He may give to you."*

How can Jesus risk such an unqualified offer as *whatever you ask?* I can quickly think of things to ask that, even if they were good, could destroy me. What if I ask that every blind person I touch would be healed—and God granted it? Could I then handle the personal obligation for the rest of my life of climbing from my bed each morning to discover hundreds, perhaps thousands of blind people standing outside my home waiting for me to touch them? How would my neighbors feel about living in complete gridlock every day? Cars and trucks and pedestrians patiently (perhaps not so patiently) waiting for my appearance to touch their blindness? It has happened before to men like William Branham. What does Jesus mean by "whatever you ask?"

In Jonesboro during the fall of 1946, William Branham stayed on the platform for eight straight days and nights, praying for a steady stream of sick and needy. He ate his meals on the platform and napped behind the pulpit while those in the prayer line stood patiently waiting for him to wake up and resume his work. By the end of the week, Branham's forehead throbbed with weariness. The backs of his hands were raw where he had pulled out the hairs, trying to keep himself awake. Still he did not want to stop. He wanted to stay there until he had prayed for every sick person who came through the doors—but he could not. The news of healings and miracles was like a magnet, drawing thousands more to Jonesboro throughout the week. When Branham finally did quit on the eighth night of that Jonesboro healing campaign, the prayer line was longer than it was when he started.[5]

I believe Christ is acknowledging the principle I call *dominion*. Because we are created in His image, we carry some power to affect the environment around us. To some degree, our world reflects what we have created, and this power comes from our internal condition of the heart.

It is clear that we receive that upon which we meditate. This is why Paul implores us to control our thoughts:

> *Phil. 4:8* *"Finally, brethren, whatever is true, whatever is honorable, whatever is right, whatever is pure, whatever is lovely, whatever is of good repute, if there is any excellence and if anything worthy of praise, dwell on these things."*

We will have what we think. If we ponder a life of chaos, one day we will discover that we live among that chaos. If we ponder a life of peace, that too we will have.

If we wish to reach God's destiny for ourselves, then we should be thinking like He thinks. We should be believing what He says. We should meditate on what is right.

Be careful here. I am not saying that we are gods. Many have followed this vain thinking beyond the boundary of scripture and created false philosophies and religious doctrines. Here, we will hold fast to God's sovereignty and absolute authority. And we will also hold fast to our humble position as stewards of Another's mission. God is divine, and we are not.

For now, let me suffice to say that death and life lie within the power of our tongue,[6] and our tongue speaks from the deep content of our heart.[7] We can learn to use this power well, or ignore it and its consequences. I will develop the principle further in Session 5—Dominion, Part A.

STEWARDSHIP

So, what is the goal of all this dreaming and prosperity of soul? Is it for our own benefit? Do we fight to get to a place of rest, and then lie down? Do we name our blessing and demand that God respond?

The right answer is love.[8] Our Master is in love with people. He carries no concern for the quality of our cars and size of our bank accounts. These material things are cultural and social measurements we fuss over. They give us a way to compare our condition with the condition of others. We measure success and failure by what we have or have not, but somehow God is not impressed with our choice of designer jeans.

It never ceases to amaze me, whenever I walk with people through financial successes and failures, how God's fingerprints can be found all over the person's heart. Regardless of the direction of change, up or down, winning or losing, the individuals privately describe their journeys and share their experiences. They share their tender dealings of the heart and it is clear that God is always attentive to building character, ever provoked by faithful action, and never moved by need.

This observation places a deep imprint into my understanding of wealth and stewardship. God is primarily interested in character and the preservation of things is always secondary. He is not afraid of separating us from possessions, for a purpose. We own nothing in this life, we are simply stewards of the people and things that God has seen fit to lend into our care. We will please Him through faithfulness, and we will do this for His glory alone.

Living our life as a trusted and faithful steward will be one of the greatest gifts we will place at our Master's feet. One day in eternity, we will present the gold refined from our lives. What are some things that you can do to build your treasure in heaven? List these in the spaces below: _____

_____

_____

_____

_____

> _Matt. 6:19-21_ "Do not store up for yourselves treasures on earth, where moth and rust destroy, and where thieves break in and steal. But store up for yourselves treasures in heaven, where neither moth nor rust destroys, and where thieves do not break in or steal; for where your treasure is, there your heart will be also."

HERMIT CRAB PROPHECIES

The hermit crab is such a funny fellow. His clumsy frame is a curious illustration of the steward. Like the steward, he is created as an unbalanced creature—one giant claw in the practical pressures of paying bills—the opposing small claw clinging to the illusive supernatural. As stewards, we diligently develop our natural skills through education and experience, and pray that God uses us in His Kingdom.

I have concluded that stewards need to switch sides. The supernatural arm must outgrow our skill and training arm. We must be more heavily balanced toward the spirit. Left to ourselves, we naturally put our claws on backwards.

If we are too naturally minded, we will become controlling and sterile. However, if we continue to dream, we avail ourselves of the supernatural. We invite the leading and designs of the Holy Spirit. We become supernatural stewards who spill vitality and miracles from our lives rather than dead compliance. We will serve the world, like Joseph did.

THE WEALTH OF CITIES

Have you ever stopped to imagine what you will do when His Kingdom comes? Will you eat grapes on cloud-couches? Or will you be a great servant to the King of kings?

I believe we will be active leaders, governors, and administrators. We will again be supernatural stewards. Consider these scriptures:

> *Luke 19:15-19* *"When he returned, after receiving the kingdom, he ordered that these slaves, to whom he had given the money, be called to him so that he might know what business they had done. The first appeared, saying, 'Master, your mina has made ten minas more.' And he said to him, 'Well done, good slave, because you have been faithful in a very little thing, you are to be in authority over ten cities.' The second came, saying, 'Your mina, master, has made five minas.' And he said to him also, 'And you are to be over five cities.'"*

The destiny of the Church is to steward great wealth. I believe that supernatural stewardship is "what's next" for the Church.

Christ is the great prize, and we will become the Bride of Christ. Our ultimate purpose is worship, and our ultimate activity is stewardship. God is moving us from glory to glory.[9]

Welcome to this great adventure. I can't wait to see what you will do!

WHAT IS POVERTY?

Poverty is a formidable foe. It has made its mark on individuals, cultures, and nations since the human story began. Today, poverty is found in every country of the world and accounts for more than eight million deaths worldwide each year.[10] It is found far from our geographic location, in struggling countries like Sudan and Haiti, and nearby in our own neighborhoods (dare I suggest—our own homes).

Consider this excerpt from Jeffrey Sachs' book, *The End of Poverty*:

> "If economic development is a ladder with higher rungs representing steps up the path to economic well-being, there are roughly one-billion people around the world, one sixth of humanity, who live as the Malawians do: too ill, hungry, or destitute even to get a foot on the first rung of the development ladder. These people are the 'poorest of the poor,' or the 'extreme poor' of the planet.
>
> A few rungs up the development ladder is the upper end of the low-income world, where roughly another 1.5 billion people face problems like those of the young women in Bangladesh. These people are 'the poor.' They live above mere subsistence. Although daily survival is pretty much assured, they struggle in the cities and countryside to make ends meet. Death is not at their door, but chronic financial hardship and a lack of basic amenities such as safe drinking water and functioning latrines are part of their daily lives. All told, the extreme poor (at around 1 billion) and the poor (another 1.5 billion) make up around 40 percent of humanity."[11]

Most of us have never experienced the grinding pain of "extreme" poverty. When faced with absolute suffering of this magnitude, it is easy to feel overwhelmed. Great men and women have formed governmental, charitable and humanitarian agencies to challenge this giant. Yet experts agree that continuing to pump endless provision into the vacuum of poverty will not solve the problem. As one lifetime missionary friend explained, it can actually cause more damage than good by creating a dependency on outsiders. If one examines the literature on global poverty, an interesting discovery is made. The antidote for extreme poverty lies in the availability of basic infrastructure (roads, power, and ports) and human capital (health and education). When these conditions are available, even in their most basic form, the marketplace is attracted—a most powerful engine for development. It is within the marketplace where the steward thrives.

SESSION THREE

MAKING THE TREE GOOD

Matt. 12:33 _"Either make the tree good and its fruit good, or make the tree bad and its fruit bad; for the tree is known by its fruit."_

SESSION OVERVIEW

Spiritual Laws Are Real

Discovery

I Just Don't Trust You

Turning Over Rocks

Rules of Roots

Raising the Sword

The Finest Rule

Final Exercise

SPIRITUAL LAWS ARE REAL

We do not question the reality of natural laws. For example, because of the effect of gravity upon us, we learn to cooperate with the law of gravity. We also learn that, by observation and experience, resisting a natural law can have unpleasant consequences—like hitting the ground if we walk off a ladder. Moreover we find that our belief in the law, or lack thereof, has no bearing whatsoever on those consequences. Spiritual laws are principles that God has set in place to order the spiritual world. Both spiritual and natural laws are invisible and both laws create an effect upon our lives. In this session, we will learn about how spiritual laws apply to a prosperous soul. We will learn to cooperate with these spiritual laws to enjoy their benefits (see Appendix 2).

Spiritual laws affect us in very real ways—even if we do not believe in those laws. Let me illustrate using the Old Testament command for tithes and offerings[1]:

> *Mal. 3:7-9* *"From the days of your fathers you have turned aside from My statutes and have not kept them. Return to Me, and I will return to you," says the LORD of hosts. "But you say, 'How shall we return?' Will a man rob God? Yet you are robbing Me! But you say, 'How have we robbed You?' In tithes and offerings. You are cursed with a curse, for you are robbing Me, the whole nation of you!"*

In those days a believer would honor God by faithfully keeping the laws of tithes and offerings. In return God confirmed His approval, in part, with protection from the devourer. In today's culture we may name the loss differently (calamity, disease, or curses) but we all understand the fruit of the "devourer."

The result of cooperation with God's laws of the tithes and offerings was directly connected to His rebuke of the devourer on the Jew's behalf:

> *Mal. 3:10-11* *"'Bring the whole tithe into the storehouse, so that there may be food in My house, and test Me now in this,' says the LORD of hosts, 'if I will not open for you the windows of heaven and pour out for you a*

blessing until it overflows. Then I will rebuke the devourer for you, so that it will not destroy the fruits of the ground; nor will your vine in the field cast its grapes,' says the LORD of hosts."

My purpose here is not to discuss whether the tithe has value under the New Testament. Instead, I want to illustrate the effect of a spiritual law upon a people. By resisting these laws, the Jews lived under a curse; by cooperating with these laws, the Jews lived under divine protection. My choice is to cooperate with spiritual laws so I can enjoy the benefits!

> *Mal. 3:12 "'All the nations will call you blessed, for you shall be a delightful land,' says the LORD of hosts.'"*

To summarize my point:

If you work "WITH" spiritual laws, they work for you.
If you work "AGAINST" spiritual laws, they work against you.

I summarize this point with the phrase, "Cooperating With Spiritual Laws."

DISCOVERY

Think of some natural and spiritual laws that you have benefited from. Think of some that you have suffered from. List these in the spaces below:

_____
_____
_____
_____
_____

Regardless of your experience, what are some spiritual laws that you would like to benefit from? List these in the spaces below:

_____
_____
_____
_____

What are some ways you could add these benefits to your life? Study the scriptures and find your own answers from God's Word.

_____

_____

_____

_____

_____

Here are a few suggestions from Proverbs:

> _Prov. 8:35_ "For he who finds wisdom finds life and obtains favor from the LORD."

> _Prov. 10:4b_ "the hand of the diligent makes rich."

> _Prov. 19:17_ "One who is gracious to a poor man lends to the LORD, and He will repay him for his good deed."

> _Prov. 20:7_ "A righteous man who walks in his integrity—how blessed are his sons after him."

Many issues will find their own remedy when we learn to cooperate with natural AND spiritual laws. Cooperating with spiritual laws is like sowing. You will reap what you sow, so sow well.

I JUST DON'T TRUST YOU

We can get lazy with our use of the English language. We use the word "believe" when we really mean, "comprehend." For example, you might say you believe that driving over the speed limit is dangerous, yet you continue to drive too quickly. It is more accurate to say that you "comprehend" the danger in speeding since your behavior does not change. Your behavior will betray what you really believe—that you are safe in your car regardless of your chosen velocity. In fact, you will find it nearly impossible to change a behavior until you adopt the underlying root as truth. It is a matter of trust. Only trust will evoke a permanent change in behavior.

Many years ago, a brave acrobat claimed that he could tightrope walk over Niagara Falls. Quickly, a crowd gathered to watch this daring feat. Slowly the acrobat climbed onto the tightrope wire and walked over the falls, spun, and returned with perfect balance and poise. Next the acrobat took a common wheelbarrow and proceeded to walk carefully along the wire. The crowd held their breath as the acrobat reversed his steps. Again, he returned safely to the land.

Turning to a young boy in the crowd, the acrobat asked if he would like to ride the wheelbarrow over the falls. Promptly, the boy replied, "No sir!" Surprised, the acrobat asked whether the boy believed he could do it. The boy replied, "Yes, I believe you can do it. I just don't trust you."

When the risk is high enough, we get our English right. The boy intuitively understood the difference between comprehension and trust. Trust is so much deeper. It is trust that gets us into the wheelbarrow. Our actions will reveal where our trust lies, regardless of our confession.

Trust is like a taproot that draws good or evil from the soil of our lives; trust permits that which lies in our heart to express itself in our lives—regardless of what we confess. This is why Jesus describes us as a branch in John 15.[2] I will summarize this second powerful idea on trust with the phrase, "Trust Begets Change."

TURNING OVER ROCKS

Develop the idea of spiritual laws in your own life. Think of some situation where your experience differs from a biblical promise. If you say that you believe the Word but fail to see its effect in your life, perhaps your English is wrong. Your comprehension of scripture will need to deepen into trust. Perhaps some behaviors will begin changing!

By combining the ideas of "cooperating with spiritual laws" and "trust begets change", we come upon a powerful opportunity. We can use these tools to change our lives; we can use these tools to experience more of the Bible's benefits.

RULES OF ROOTS

Take a good look at your fruit (thoughts, feelings, habits, etc.). What does your internal dialog repeatedly say to you? What do your feelings about wealth and money reveal about what you believe? What are your contradictory behaviors and secret battles? Consider these examples:

<u>Fruit:</u> "Money petrifies me with fear".
<u>Root:</u> "God is weaker than my capacity for failure."

<u>Fruit:</u> "I feel guilty about having money."
<u>Root:</u> "God doesn't like rich Christians."

<u>Fruit:</u> "I'm selfish with my money."
<u>Root:</u> "There is not enough money to go around. I might have to go without."

When evaluating fruits and roots, be aware of the first rule of roots: Only good fruit comes from good roots; only bad fruit comes from bad roots. This is Bible. One cannot come from the other.

> *Matt. 7:17-19* "*So every good tree bears good fruit, but the bad tree bears bad fruit. A good tree cannot produce bad fruit, nor can a bad tree produce good fruit.*"

Begin to examine your own fruit right now. List several personal examples of bad fruit in your life. For this moment, limit your scope to finances (although these principles go far beyond money). Follow each fruit with the underlying untruth. Ask God to help you.

Bad Fruit:_____

_____

Root Lie:_____

_____

Bad Fruit:_____

_____

Root Lie:_____

_____

Bad Fruit:_____

_____

Root Lie:_____

_____

Repeat this prayer with me:

"Father God, I am your child. I gave my life to you on _____(list the date of your salvation). You have proven Your faithful goodness to generations before me, and You again will show Your goodness to me right now.

"I need Your grace to discover the lies I have trusted and I ask you now to show them to me."

Take a few more moments to finish what God is revealing. Be honest. Be brave.

RAISING THE SWORD

As you uncover deep lies embedded in your belief system, you may feel strong emotions. This is because your soul is facing a crisis. When you embrace things to be true and later discover those things to be lies, you can feel fear, confusion, discouragement, or even anger. You may be tempted to protect yourself and not change. The lies have created a false sense of safety. The lies have become familiar spirits.

Can you feel the tension building? We have taken up the sword of truth and are preparing to sever roots deeply grounded in lies.

Before we raise the sword, I will share the second rule of roots: If you sever a root, the fruit will die. Events and circumstances could change right now. This is the very purpose of Christ on the cross, to sever the root of sin. Cut those lies off and you will succeed in the process of prosperity. You are raising the sword!

Again, take a few more moments to finish what God is revealing.

Place your hand over your list of root lies. Repeat this prayer with me:

"Father God, I recognize that these lies create destructive forces in my life. I recognize that You did not teach me these things, but I have learned them from people and events from my past.

"I forgive those people now. I forgive _____(quietly speak their names as God brings them to your mind) and release him/her into Your hand.

"I forsake those events now. I forgive myself for _____(quietly renounce events in your past as God brings them to your mind) and release those into Your hand.

"I ask you, Father, to strike these lies at the root and sever their effect in my life, my family's history, and my family's future.

"Finally, Father, I ask you to replace each of these lies with biblical truth. Occupy my heart with Your Word. Improve my soil and bless my destiny of a prosperous soul. Bless my family tree with abundant life. Amen."

Now your prophetic act. Perform this over your list of root lies:

"I sever, by faith in Jesus Christ, the root lie of _____ right now."

Repeat this prayer for every lie God has shown you. Continue until every one has been addressed.

Once you have done this prayer for each lie, take a few moments and write out some of your thoughts and emotions. Turn this into a personal declaration of independence. _____

_____

_____

_____

_____

_____

_____

_____

_____

_____

THE FINEST RULE

Until now, we have been concentrating on extricating and severing lies. But there is a final rule of roots: Sowing will produce new fruit. You will plant new roots by sowing seeds of truth into your heart. These seeds, as promised, will produce good fruit many times over.

Proverbs promises that things we labor over will produce a return. Look at Proverbs 14:23.[3] Laboring for good will have the effect of gain. It is tending the garden of our heart that produces a prosperous soul.

Jesus told us to make the tree good. Good fruit is our responsibility.

> *Matt. 12:33* "*Either make the tree good and its fruit good, or make the tree bad and its fruit bad; for the tree is known by its fruit.*"

Changing what I trust will change my experience. Changing what I trust can make the tree good. This is key to exchanging the spirit of poverty for a prosperous soul.

PROPHETIC EXERCISE

Quickly list your root lies that the Holy Spirit has shown you onto a stickie. Use as many stickies as you need.

As a final act, bring your "lie" stickies to the white board and leave them behind. As you do this, speak this prophetic utterance, "I am making my tree good."

Tonight, take out a U. S. coin or bill, and read the inscription, "In God We Trust." Begin to plant your new seeds of truths. Be open with your new ideas and share them with others. Do not be secretive or afraid to test them against scripture and counsel. All plants grow best in light. Welcome to prosperity!

My New Seeds of Truth: _____

_____

_____

_____

_____

Touch your head and say, "I am a prosperous soul."

SESSION FOUR

BREAKING THE SPIRIT OF POVERTY

Proverbs 23:7a "For as he thinks within himself, so he is."

A FOREIGN LANGUAGE

Every community or culture develops its own language and customs, and Christianity is no exception. Consider our common usage of the phrase, "poverty spirit." What do you think of the phrase? How would you explain it to someone from another culture?_____

_____

_____

_____

_____

NEED TO KNOW

As introduction to this class, I made the following statement:

> "The second goal of this class is breakthrough. For those who suffer under a poverty spirit, I seek the destruction of that evil stronghold. For those who already walk in freedom, I seek promotion, advancement, and increase. Idle talk about the concepts of a poverty spirit and a prosperous soul hold no interest for me; the Bible warns us away from mere speculation.[1] My second goal is, simply put, the invasion of a supernatural heaven into a natural world. 'On earth as it is in heaven.' If this class enables you to begin or advance your own prosperity of soul, then we both have succeeded."

The biblical concept of knowledge is deeper than the mere gathering of facts: it implies that a person has gained experience with the subject of study. A person who gains knowledge in law has studied and practiced in the field before they claim to be knowledgeable. As stewards, we accept that it is not enough to learn about money and business and financing strategies. The steward will grow into the calling. This requires the courage to change. To be a success, a steward must live and serve from a genuine place of knowledge. In the context of prosperity, it would be a failure to teach and minister about a prosperous soul and, deep down, not be enjoying that same experience ourselves. We want to live out of what we know. Like the apostle John, we must teach what we know:

> *1John 1:1-3* "*What was from the beginning, what we have heard, what we have seen with our eyes, what we have looked at and touched with our hands, concerning the Word of Life—and the life was manifested, and we have seen and testify and proclaim to you the eternal life, which was with the Father and was manifested to us—what we have seen and heard we proclaim to you also, so that you too may have fellowship with us; and indeed our fellowship is with the Father, and with His Son Jesus Christ.*"

John taught what he knew to be true. He handled and observed things in Christ's daily life, which he handed down through time. Likewise, we will steward from our experience of a prosperous soul.

At this point, I want to address a "fear" of knowledge. Valuing and pursuing knowledge as a Christian was one of my first challenges. As I have pursued my own prosperous soul, I have had to face the risk of stumbling into pride. Knowledge is power. And knowledge puffs us up!

> *1Cor. 8:1b* "*Knowledge makes arrogant, but love edifies.*"

This is the challenge of the steward: to not be afraid of powerful things, but rise above them for Christ's sake, bringing His Kingdom to earth. If we are afraid of power, or if we abuse it, we are bowing to a poverty spirit. These are like cracks in one's foundation. When the weightier things begin to build upon a cracked foundation, one cannot help but fail. If our soul is prosperous, we will act powerfully for Christ, in fearless love.

WHAT A POVERTY SPIRIT IS

We will begin our definition of a "poverty spirit" by understanding the word *spirit*. In scripture, the word *spirit* usually comes from the word *ruach* (Hebrew) and *pneuma* (Greek), meaning breath, wind, or spirit.

The phrase "poverty spirit" is not a scriptural phrase. A word study will reveal "poverty" and "spirit" used independently, but never linked. So, what are we talking about when we speak of a spirit of poverty?

A Bible word study on "poverty" is very revealing. You will discover that scripture describes poverty as a possession.

> *Prov. 10:15* *"The rich man's wealth is his fortress, the ruin of the poor is their poverty."*

> *Prov. 24:34* *"Then your poverty will come as a robber and your want like an armed man."*

> *Prov. 31:7* *"Let him drink and forget his poverty and remember his trouble no more."*

Scripture reflects the possessive nature of a person with a poverty spirit. Understand that poverty is a thing that people hold closely, in spite of its destructive nature. Some people will even fight to keep it. Some will fight to drag others down who are climbing out. Poverty is possessive.

Before we continue, think about how poverty has affected your life. Write some brief comments on how you see poverty has or is shaping you today.

_____

_____

_____

_____

_____

_____

Finally, we will disempower the idea that a devil named *Poverty* is attacking you. Instead, consider poverty as an aerial influence or a television channel that you tune to and agree with. Demons are real, but they are no match for a follower of Christ. This is an important point since some people consider their poverty to be a personal and inevitable harassment by the devil. This is a victim mentality—a cousin to the poverty mentality.

If a poverty spirit was a demon, Christians would pray and cast the poverty out of a person based on their authority in Christ. Christ told us to perform supernatural acts that included casting out demons. Demons are under our authority.

> *Matt. 10:8* "*Heal the sick, raise the dead, cleanse the lepers, cast out demons. Freely you received, freely give.*"

Have you ever noticed that, regardless of how we pray, we cannot cast out a spirit of poverty? This is because a poverty spirit is not a demon: it is a mindset or an attitude. I believe the spirit we encounter most often is the biblical position of a *power* from Ephesians 6:

> *Eph. 6:12* "*For our struggle is not against flesh and blood, but against the rulers, against the powers, against the world forces of this darkness, against the spiritual forces of wickedness in the heavenly places.*"

In Francis Frangipane's book entitled *The Three Battlegrounds*, he describes demons as the ground troops of hell. He goes on to describe a *power* as an evil energy that broadcasts like radio waves over a territory.

Consider Frangipane's strategy to defeating a *power*:

> "*the means through which the church successfully wars against Powers is through the administration of Christ's spiritual authority and the principle of displacement. Powers are not "cast out", they are displaced in the spirit-realm by the fullness of the reign of Christ in the church, and through the intercessory warfare of the saints in the region.*"[2]

> *2Cor. 10:4-5* "*for the weapons of our warfare are not of the flesh, but divinely powerful for the destruction of fortresses. We are destroying speculations and every lofty thing raised up against the knowledge of God, and we are taking every thought captive to the obedience of Christ.*"

Take a moment and consider who you listen to. Consider how you and others speak of their life. Are those voices faith-filled and hopeful? Are they pessimistic and discouraging? Write down some of your observations. What action will you take?

_____

_____

_____

_____

_____

We know that damage occurs when we *agree* with a lying spirit. The Bible is clear about the potency of our thoughts. A poverty spirit can become our view of the world. It can become our paradigm, an expectation of evil.

Stephen Covey describes a paradigm as a perspective or a predetermined viewpoint.[3] Pessimism and worry are both paradigms of a poverty spirit. A paradigm is like a map, showing an overview of our world. A poverty map will illustrate impassable routes (lack, doubt, decrease, loss). If the poverty map is replaced with a prosperity map, your paradigm changes. Now you see the bridges, roads, and mountain passes. You have experienced a paradigm shift.

Paradigm shifts are very important and cannot be understated. In fact, every major historic advance in human history has come as a result of a paradigm shift.

> _Proverbs 23:7a_ *"For as he thinks within himself, so he is."*

DIRTY PRINTS

Have you ever handled many newspapers, turned to something else, and discovered that your hands have become blackened by ink? You see your prints everywhere, like an inky trail of what your hands have touched. So, too, does a poverty spirit leave an inky history.

1. A poverty spirit fights to keep you, and causes you to keep others, in the

same condition. If someone has a breakthrough in their investments or finances, it is the poverty spirit that hopes they lose it, or at least counts the reasons why they will lose it all again.

2. A poverty spirit hounds you. It steals your peace. You feel chased by trouble. You feel helpless. Money flees from you.

3. A poverty spirit hides you. You find yourself overlooked and ignored. You should be seen-and-not-heard. You believe your opinion is irrelevant.

4. A poverty spirit creates anxiety (a nice word for fear). Your stomach turns when you enter a parking lot, because you are afraid you will not get a parking spot. You rush to a sale, worried that you will miss the last item.

5. A poverty spirit hordes and accumulates junk. You save the fast-food restaurant plastic cup collection. A poverty spirit looks like the narrow path in your garage because you save everything you and your parents ever broke.

6. A poverty spirit "settles" when it should fight. It is the powerless feeling when we dream about something. It looks like the unwillingness to press through challenges. It is the conviction that "things just happen to me." It is passive victimization.

7. A poverty spirit reaches for instant gratification. It is the impulse purchase. You spend thousands on trinkets, yet resist a plan to purchase quality. This goes for investing also.

8. A poverty spirit feels out of control. You feel that your finances rule you. You feel enslaved or trapped. You believe that you are powerless.

9. A poverty spirit chokes out generosity. Generosity is an inevitable outcome for the prosperous soul. Pastor Bill Johnson says that tithing is the kindergarten of a Christian life. The result of prosperity and wealth MUST be radical generosity.

Again, take a moment and write down any other fingerprints that you see in your life. _____

_____

_____

_____

_____

_____

_____

_____

WHAT A POVERTY SPIRIT IS NOT

A poverty spirit is not an economic problem. It is easy to believe that "it takes money to make money" (another poverty fingerprint). I believe, like Joseph, a prosperous soul will always lift you, and a poverty spirit will always sink you. Consider how many people you know of that are miserable. (The word miserable comes from the Latin *miserari*, 'to pity,' and from *miser*, 'wretched.') You will find miserable people on either side of riches—those who have excess, and those who have lack. Poverty is not about money.

I have found that people can be rich and miserable. And I found that people can be poor and miserable. So, when someone chooses to be miserable, they do so regardless of their financial statements. They might as well be rich!

Sometimes, we confuse hard work or struggle with the poverty mentality. Working toward a goal that takes perseverance and determination is often (usually) very hard work. I have never heard of a financial success that has not required the person to answer the difficult challenge of growth and change. Living in wealth is hard work, make no mistake. Scripture is clear too—hasty gain grows wings.

> Prov. 28:20 "A faithful man will abound with blessings, but he who makes haste to be rich will not go unpunished."

Don't confuse hard work and hardship with the poverty mentality. Hard work is noble, prosperous. Hardship is circumstantial, temporary. Neither will unconditionally identify the presence of a poverty spirit working in your life.

Americans have lived so well for so long that we have come to expect ease of living. Many of us complain about everything: our coffee is too hot, our meals too cold. However, it takes very little effort to discover that this is not the common experience of human history. We will be naïve and arrogant to think that ease is a supernatural right that we can pray in. This assumption makes much of our evangelistic message irrelevant to the world. Hard work and hardship are common parts of life and often keys to our maturity as believers. Consider the saying, "Calm seas do not make good sailors."

> *1Pet. 4:12-13* "Beloved, do not be surprised at the fiery ordeal among you, which comes upon you for your testing, as though some strange thing were happening to you; but to the degree that you share the sufferings of Christ, keep on rejoicing, so that also at the revelation of His glory you may rejoice with exultation."

Finally, even failure does not confirm a poverty spirit. There is no guarantee of success when we stamp "God said" on an idea or plan. Most financial problems I have seen are caused by honest mistakes and poor decisions. These are simply lessons from life and not spiritual matters at all.

WHAT A PROSPEROUS SOUL IS

I think a prosperous soul is more easily observed than defined but here are some of my reflections.

1. A prosperous soul is our privilege as citizens of heaven. Read these verses anew, in light of a prosperous soul.

Proverbs 10:22 "It is the blessing of the LORD that makes rich, and He adds no sorrow to it."

Proverbs 25:2 "It is the glory of God to conceal a matter, but the glory of kings is to search out a matter."

Deut. 8:18 "But you shall remember the LORD your God, for it is He who is giving you power to make wealth, that He may confirm His covenant which He swore to your fathers, as it is this day."

2. A prosperous soul is correct thinking, releasing the promises of God on our behalf. Read the following verses and imagine these powerful verses acting in your daily living. What would your life resemble if you were "filled with the knowledge of His will?" How far could you go if you were "bearing fruit in every good work?"

Col. 1:9-13 "For this reason also, since the day we heard of it, we have not ceased to pray for you and to ask that you may be filled with the knowledge of His will in all spiritual wisdom and understanding, so that you will walk in a manner worthy of the Lord, to please Him in all respects, bearing fruit in every good work and increasing in the knowledge of God; strengthened with all power, according to His glorious might, for the attaining of all steadfastness and patience; joyously giving thanks to the Father, who has qualified us to share in the inheritance of the saints in Light. For He rescued us from the domain of darkness, and transferred us to the kingdom of His beloved Son… "

3. A prosperous soul has dominion over one's things. Things serve people, not the other way around. Money becomes the servant, a powerful tool when used (stewarded) for His purposes.

Gen. 50:19-21 "But Joseph said to them, 'Do not be afraid, for am I in God's place? As for you, you meant evil against me, but God meant it for good in order to bring about this present result, to preserve many people alive. So therefore, do not be afraid; I will provide for you and your little ones.' So, he comforted them and spoke kindly to them."

WHAT A PROSPEROUS SOUL IS NOT

As with anything of worth or power, there is the possibility for abuse. When you add something as emotive as prosperity, the risk becomes so much greater. Some Bible teachers of the past have emphasized narrow aspects of the Bible to demonstrate God's generous intentions. These men and women carried decades of understanding into their message. Then, as younger teachers picked up the elders' messages, the message was taken out of context and beyond what is true. These distortions became abusive and damaging to the cause of Christ. The secular world saw right through it, as we do now also.

The purpose of a prosperous soul is not for ourselves, although we will benefit. The purpose must be for the advancement of Christ and His Kingdom. God cares nothing of things, only people. If we keep Christ first and "others" as our focus, we will go far in stewarding well.

> *Matt. 25:21* *"His master said to him, 'Well done, good and faithful slave. You were faithful with a few things, I will put you in charge of many things; enter into the joy of your master.'"*

A prosperous soul is not always "more" and "bigger". Prosperity includes contentment, simplicity, and sacrifice. How much more prosperous is a person when they sacrifice a thing for someone else's benefit! This is the root of generosity.

> *Acts 20:35* *"In everything I showed you that by working hard in this manner you must help the weak and remember the words of the Lord Jesus, that He Himself said, 'It is more blessed to give than to receive.'"*

A prosperous soul is not a license for carelessness over money. As you learn to think and behave from a prosperous soul, learn stewardship and purpose. I have seen people spending money they did not have and giving away "bread and seed" in the name of generosity. I call this the "Johnny Appleseed Syndrome". Sowing seed makes good sense; sowing bread makes a mess.

Prov. 27:23 *"Know well the condition of your flocks, and pay attention to your herds…"*

2Cor. 9:7 *"Each one must do just as he has purposed in his heart, not grudgingly or under compulsion, for God loves a cheerful giver."*

A prosperous soul does not strive or worry about money. Scripture is clear that provision is God's job, not ours. Pursue wealth, and remember that money is only a small part of wealth. See Appendix Wealth handout.

Prov. 23:4 *"Do not weary yourself to gain riches, cease from your consideration of it. When you set your eyes on it, it is gone. For it certainly makes itself wings like an eagle that flies toward the heavens."*

GLORY TO GLORY

One final characteristic of a prosperous soul is the progression from self-control, to freedom, to liberty. This is an application of the spiritual law of glory to glory:

2Cor. 3:18 *"But we all, with unveiled face, beholding as in a mirror the glory of the Lord, are being transformed into the same image from glory to glory, just as from the Lord, the Spirit."*

Freedom is the *absence* of restraint. Liberty, however, is the *presence* of the power to choose between alternatives rather than merely be unrestrained. As we mature, we discover that something of absence (freedom) is replaced by something of presence (liberty). In God's Kingdom, we are always moving from good to better to best. We are moving from one glory to another glory, always increasing.

EXERCISE

Think about the fingerprints and characteristics discussed above. Pray whether you see any "bent" in your life toward a poverty spirit. In scripture, the word *bent* literally means "to hang". Any bent toward poverty will eventually hang you. It is good to break the effect of this spirit in your life right now. As a prophetic act, straighten a paper clip and observe the bends that cannot be made right. Take a moment and write a brief list of your poverty bents you wish to break. Work the open paper clip until it actually breaks.

_____

_____

_____

_____

_____

_____

_____

_____

_____

Place your broken token in your hand and repeat this prayer with me:

"Father God, thank you for revealing my bents toward poverty. I recognize that these are lies designed to wreck Your purpose for my life. I want these removed and replaced with truth right now. Take these away and displace every spirit of error with Your Spirit of Truth.

"Father, I receive my prosperous soul, in Jesus' name. Amen."

> *1 Chronicles 4:10* "*Now Jabez called on the God of Israel, saying, 'Oh that You would bless me indeed and enlarge my border, and that Your hand might be with me, and that You would keep me from harm that it may not pain me!' And God granted him what he requested.*"

Touch your head and say, "I am a prosperous soul."

SESSION FIVE

DOMINION, PART A

Prov. 13:12 "*Hope deferred makes the heart sick, but desire fulfilled is a tree of life.*"

Rev. 22:1-2 "*Then he showed me a river of the water of life, clear as crystal, coming from the throne of God and of the Lamb, in the middle of its street. On either side of the river was the tree of life, bearing twelve kinds of fruit, yielding its fruit every month; and the leaves of the tree were for the healing of the nations.*"

SESSION OVERVIEW

Tree of Life

Casting Seed

Perfect Theology

Catch a Glimpse

Dominion Turning

TREE OF LIFE

This session is about finding the Tree of Life. Most of us think of the Tree of Life as something ancient and forbidden. Genesis chapters 2 and 3 describe Adam and Eve's error. They snuck a bite from the Tree of Knowledge, against God's direction. Every tree but one was permitted for food. (I wonder what the fruit from the other trees would offer. Perhaps a Tree of Joy? Was there a Tree of Laughter or a Tree of Contentment…?) In the garden every tree was good, and they were all available; only one was forbidden—the Tree of Knowledge. God knew that once humankind ate the fruit of knowledge, we would become accountable to God because of our knowledge. Even the Tree of Life was not forbidden until man "knew" sin. In His mercy, God protected us from the Tree of Life in a sin-fallen state. It is likely that eating from the Tree of Life after falling into sin would have locked us into a state of eternal separation from God, unable to benefit from the ultimate sacrifice, Jesus Christ, the Lamb of God. God placed a serious obstacle to the Tree of Life, and hid the gate to the Garden. He set in place a plan for redemption: a Savior would be given for us.

> *Gen. 3:24* *"So He drove the man out; and at the east of the garden of Eden He stationed the cherubim and the flaming sword which turned every direction to guard the way to the tree of life."*

We see the tree again in Revelation 22, only this time it is planted in the New Jerusalem. With heaven touching earth, we see an amazing illustration from John the Revelator:

> *Rev. 22:1-2* *"Then he showed me a river of the water of life, clear as crystal, coming from the throne of God and of the Lamb, in the middle of its street. On either side of the river was the tree of life, bearing twelve kinds of fruit, yielding its fruit every month; and the leaves of the tree were for the healing of the nations."*

Here we see this beautiful illustration of crystal-clear purity, continual fruitfulness, and healing of nations. The Bible again places the Tree of Life out of reach until some future time, the new heaven and new earth.

Nestled between Genesis and Revelation are the words of the wisest man to ever live. Solomon spoke about the Tree of Life in verse, as a prophetic declaration for us today:

> *Prov. 13:12* *"Hope deferred makes the heart sick, but desire fulfilled is a tree of life."*

Here, Solomon is prophesying Jesus Christ, the Desire of the Nations.[1]

CASTING SEED

We have been looking closely at seed and fruit, trust and lies, poverty and prosperity. At this point let's look at money and identify the seeds that will produce good and powerful fruit in your life.

Write down some truths that you believe about money. Look for the good seed at this point. _____

_____

_____

_____

_____

_____

Money is not a curse and God uses money to bless people. He will use money to bless you, too. Here are some things to consider:

1. You are blessed through Adam and Eve, when God promised abundance, authority, and dominion.

> *Gen. 1:28* *"God blessed them; and God said to them, 'Be fruitful and multiply, and fill the earth, and subdue it; and rule over the fish of the sea and over the birds of the sky and over every living thing that moves on the earth.'"*

2. You are blessed through the Jews (we are spiritual Jews), when God blessed their escape from captivity and settlement into their own land with wealth and riches.

> *Isaiah 61:6-7* *"But you will be called the priests of the LORD; You will be spoken of as ministers of our God. You will eat the wealth of nations, and in their riches you will boast. Instead of your shame you will have a double portion, and instead of humiliation they will shout for joy over their portion. Therefore they will possess a double portion in their land, everlasting joy will be theirs."*

3. You are blessed through Abraham, when God blessed Abraham in every way.

> *Gen. 24:1* *"Now Abraham was old, advanced in age; and the LORD had blessed Abraham in every way."*

> *Gen. 24:35* *"The LORD has greatly blessed my master Abraham, so that he has become rich; and He has given him flocks and herds, and silver and gold, and servants and maids, and camels and donkeys."*

> *Gal. 3:14* *"in order that in Christ Jesus the blessing of Abraham might come to the Gentiles, so that we would receive the promise of the Spirit through faith."*

4. You are blessed through Job, when God granted Job fortune.

> *Job 1:10* *"Have You not made a hedge about him and his house and all that he has, on every side? You have blessed the work of his hands, and his possessions have increased in the land."*

> *Job 42:10* *"The LORD restored the fortunes of Job when he prayed for his friends, and the LORD increased all that Job had twofold."*

5. You are blessed through Obed-edom (as worshipers of God), when God gave Obed-edom "things".

2Sam. 6:12 "*Now it was told King David, saying, 'The LORD has blessed the house of Obed-edom and all that belongs to him, on account of the ark of God.' David went and brought up the ark of God from the house of Obed-edom into the city of David with gladness.*"

6. You are blessed through David, when God established David's throne forever.

   1Kings 2:45b "*...and the throne of David shall be established before the LORD forever.*"

7. You are blessed through Solomon, when God blessed Solomon with riches a honor.

   1Kings 3:13 "*I have also given you what you have not asked, both riches and honor, so that there will not be any among the kings like you all your days.*"

8. You are blessed through the early Christians, when God blessed those believers for their generosity.

   Phil. 4:17 "*Not that I seek the gift itself, but I seek for the profit which increases to your account.*"

   2Cor. 9:5 "*So I thought it necessary to urge the brethren that they would go on ahead to you and arrange beforehand your previously promised bountiful gift, so that the same would be ready as a bountiful gift and not affected by covetousness.*"

   1Tim. 6:17 "*Instruct those who are rich in this present world not to be conceited or to fix their hope on the uncertainty of riches, but on God, who richly supplies us with all things to enjoy.*"

9. You are blessed through righteous-living believers, when God blessed them with the right to the tree of life.

Rev. 22:14 "*Blessed are those who wash their robes, so that they may have the right to the tree of life, and may enter by the gates into the city.*"

My point is that God uses money to bless people, and those blessings are relevant to you and I today. What are some examples of God's blessing you with money in your life? Write them down as a "stone of remembrance."

_____
_____
_____
_____
_____
_____
_____

PERFECT THEOLOGY

Christ is perfect theology. By grace, we will be as He was, doing what He did.

Psa. 145:13 "*Your kingdom is an everlasting kingdom, and Your dominion endures throughout all generations.*"

God lives in dominion and He created us for that same purpose:

Gen. 1:28 "*God blessed them; and God said to them, 'Be fruitful and multiply, and fill the earth, and subdue it; and rule over the fish of the sea and over the birds of the sky and over every living thing that moves on the earth.'*"

Dominion is defined by the Oxford American dictionary as *sovereignty* or *control*. What is dominion? Describe dominion in your own words. _____

_____
_____
_____
_____
_____

The goal is not more money or more possessions. Rather, it should be "dominion over" ourselves and things. Money serves us and we serve God. Look at this example of our perfect role model, Jesus Christ.

> *Mark 4:37-41* "*And there arose a fierce gale of wind, and the waves were breaking over the boat so much that the boat was already filling up. Jesus Himself was in the stern, asleep on the cushion; and they woke Him and said to Him, 'Teacher, do You not care that we are perishing?' And He got up and rebuked the wind and said to the sea, 'Hush, be still.' And the wind died down and it became perfectly calm. And He said to them, 'Why are you afraid? Do you still have no faith?' They became very much afraid and said to one another, 'Who then is this, that even the wind and the sea obey Him?'*"

I believe that because we are created in His image, we are always expressing dominion. We create our environment around us. Dominion is created by us. To some degree, our world reflects what we have created. We create out of our internal condition.

Please do not take this thought beyond my example. This has already been done, with sad consequences. Do not create a doctrine out of something that is intended merely to illustrate a narrow principle—the principle of dominion. Some authors have called this the "Law of Attraction" and gone on to vainly imagine themselves as gods. This was the same pride that tempted Lucifer.

Pastor Bill Johnson was teaching on dominion and touched on the point I wish to make here. Here is an excerpt from that message[2]:

> "*Israel wandered in the desert for 40 years. Hebrews 3 says that they wandered in their hearts first. Their internal reality of confusion, chaos, divided focus, that which was in them, defined the nature of the world around them. People who get born-again, try their best to live for God, tithe, give offerings, come to church every week, but have fear and anxiety in here [their heart], always reproduce that in their home. And create a generation of young people who grow up in conflict and in stress because the internal reality of the parent became the external reality in their home.*

"So, when he [Jesus] stood at the edge of the boat [Mark 4:39], He was literally releasing His personal experience over a storm. You have authority over any storm you can sleep in. Jesus Christ was modeling what Paul would later get language for, being seated in heavenly places in Christ. Paul got language for Jesus' experience. As Jesus came from the realm of the perfect dominion of God, confronting the storm, he was able to release his personal experience; the storm yielded. Jesus is modeling the Christian life.

"I believe in prayer, I believe in answers to prayer, but I'll tell you that I am more convinced all the time that the lifestyle of prayer is for the purpose of encounter so that the encounter you received is the encounter you can impart."

We recreate the environment around us from what is inside of us. I call this the law of dominion. Describe some storms that you face that are requiring you to "get bigger." What storms is God highlighting to you?

_____

_____

_____

_____

_____

CATCH A GLIMPSE

I will illustrate "dominion" with some real-life examples. When we are in dominion, we are comfortable with possession. Possession is a tool, not an identity. Our identity remains securely in Christ and we are comfortable living in the role of a steward.

When we are in dominion, we are the head and not the tail. We are unafraid of responsibility, authority, and leadership because perfect love casts out fear. We recognize the great challenge and this turns us to prayer. Our motive is love, not fear.

Deuteronomy 28:13 "The LORD will make you the head and not the tail, and you only will be above, and you will not be underneath, if you listen to the commandments of the LORD your God, which I charge you today, to observe them carefully."

When we are in dominion, we are growing and increasing—because we have been given the power to increase. We look for God's natural and supernatural opportunities and act upon them. We are not passive in our role, but active. Faith is an action word.

Deuteronomy 8:18 "But you shall remember the LORD your God, for it is He who is giving you power to make wealth, that He may confirm His covenant which He swore to your fathers, as it is this day."

When we are in dominion, we will possess and influence things and others. As a mature man/woman of God, we are expected to be teachers, accustomed to "solid food" rather than milk.

1Cor. 3:2 "I gave you milk to drink, not solid food; for you were not yet able to receive it. Indeed, even now you are not yet able... "

Heb. 5:12 "For though by this time you ought to be teachers, you have need again for someone to teach you the elementary principles of the oracles of God, and you have come to need milk and not solid food."

Heb. 5:14 "But solid food is for the mature, who because of practice have their senses trained to discern good and evil."

When we are in dominion, we will demonstrate patience and self-control. We will bear the fruits of the Spirit in our life.

Gal. 5:22-23 "But the fruit of the Spirit is love, joy, peace, patience, kindness, goodness, faithfulness, gentleness, self-control; against such things there is no law."

Phil. 4:6-7 *"Be anxious for nothing, but in everything by prayer and supplication with thanksgiving let your requests be made known to God. And the peace of God, which surpasses all comprehension, will guard your hearts and your minds in Christ Jesus."*

When we are in dominion, our actions spring from faith (the expectation of good) rather than fear (the expectation of evil). Even our common actions become supernatural because the actions issue from faith.

Acts 10:31 *"and he said, 'Cornelius, your prayer has been heard and your alms have been remembered before God.'"*

Heb. 11:6 *"And without faith it is impossible to please Him, for he who comes to God must believe that He is and that He is a rewarder of those who seek Him."*

When we are in dominion, our actions reflect our Master. We resemble a prince/princess instead of a pauper. We are defined by our acts of honor, humility, and character. Dominion is a posture of authority.

Prov. 29:2 *"When the righteous increase, the people rejoice, but when a wicked man rules, people groan."*

DOMINION TURNING

Finally, when we are in dominion, we are like one who faces into a river. Facing upstream, God's good gifts approach us. We are standing in a posture of faith with an expectation of good. Remember that we do not control what comes down the river. That would be God's job.

We are about to experience a powerful prayer. Many people have had their lives changed by this experience. I will hand you the tool and I am excited to hear how God uses it in each of your lives.

Proverbs 29:18a says, "Where there is no vision, the people are unrestrained…".

The word *vision* comes from a root that means to behold, or envision, or to prophesy. Hebrews 5:14 describes the mature as those "who because of practice have their senses trained to discern good and evil." I will prophesy, and you will practice training your senses. Close your eyes. Imagine yourself standing in a river. Let me describe the river by quoting from Revelation 22:

> *Rev. 22:1-5* "*Then he showed me a river of the water of life, clear as crystal, coming from the throne of God and of the Lamb, in the middle of its street. On either side of the river was the tree of life, bearing twelve kinds of fruit, yielding its fruit every month; and the leaves of the tree were for the healing of the nations. There will no longer be any curse; and the throne of God and of the Lamb will be in it, and His bond-servants will serve Him; they will see His face, and His name will be on their foreheads. And there will no longer be any night; and they will not have need of the light of a lamp nor the light of the sun, because the Lord God will illumine them; and they will reign forever and ever.*"

You are facing downstream. God is placing good things into the crystal river for you. Yet you are a spectator, watching good things float past you just out of reach.

Wait here for God to show you this picture. You are envisioning.

Pray this aloud:

"I am standing in the crystal river of time.
This river is flowing from the throne of God and of the Lamb.
God fills the river with good things.
Because I am facing downstream,
good things flow away from me.
They are just beyond my reach, too hard to catch."

Pause until you envision this perspective. When you can imagine the scene, continue praying aloud:

"Lord Jesus, I want to turn. I want to see Your throne,
I want to see your provision.
I turn around, in Jesus' name."

Turn around to face the opposite direction. Again, pause until you can envision the new perspective. When you can imagine the Scene, continue praying aloud:

"I am facing upstream.
I can see the throne of God and the Lamb.

"Good things are coming to me.
The good things are everywhere, here in the river.

"There's more than I can contain,
there is abundance here for everyone. Even me.

"Amen."

Place your river rock token into your memorial bag at home. You will encounter new thoughts and circumstances now. You will need to develop new habits. Next session, we will look into some ideas about "facing upstream." Between now and then, take some time to pray and ask God about your turn. Practice facing upstream. Look, listen, smell, taste, feel. Describe it. Write out your testimony of what God is showing you.

_____

_____

_____

_____

_____

_____

_____

_____

_____

_____

_____

Touch your head and say, "I am a prosperous soul."

SESSION SIX

DOMINION, PART B

Rev. 22:1-2 *"Then he showed me a river of the water of life, clear as crystal, coming from the throne of God and of the Lamb."*

Heb. 11:6 *"And without faith it is impossible to please Him, for he who comes to God must believe that He is and that He is a rewarder of those who seek Him."*

SESSION OVERVIEW

Rewarder

New Practices

Lesson #1

Lesson #2

Lesson #3

Exercises

REWARDER

Look back to last week's outline. The last page provided space to describe what you saw. Review this page and share with the class what you saw. Saying it out loud will serve to reinforce the experience. Can you believe that God really showed you something? This will require your faith. Do you believe that God could do this?

> *Heb. 11:6* *"And without faith it is impossible to please Him, for he who comes to God must believe that He is and that He is a rewarder of those who seek Him."*

Again, envision the river. Time is flowing toward you from the throne. There is no limitation, no lack. God places good things in the river, for you and for your friends. Good things flow toward you. They are easy to catch. They are placed there for you. Can you believe that?

I believe that returning to this experience (in the river) is what Hebrews 5 refers to as "having our senses trained." I have room in my theology for God to act personally and powerfully in my life. It is an expression of my faith. You, too, can practice as the author of Hebrews suggests:

> *Heb. 5:14* *"But solid food is for the mature, who because of practice have their senses trained to discern good and evil."*

Consider this new paradigm from the river. The river is crystal clear, coming from the throne of God and of the Lamb. As you stand in this river and look up-stream, you will look forward to seeing your good things available in the river. You can risk believing because of the foundations that heaven is built upon. Pastor Bill Johnson calls these foundations the four Pillars of Heaven[1]:

God is in a good mood	*[The nature of God]*
Nothing is impossible	*[The nature of the testimony]*
Christ's victory is complete	*[The nature of Christ]*
I am significant	*[The nature of you]*

Can you believe in the character of heaven? Let's look at each pillar. Write down your reactions to these powerful ideas. Discuss each of them with your group:

God is in a good mood. I can rest and receive because of the nature of God:

> *1John 1:5* *"This is the message we have heard from Him and announce to you, that God is Light, and in Him there is no darkness at all."*

> *Is. 65:22-24* *"They will not build and another inhabit, they will not plant and another eat; for as the lifetime of a tree, so will be the days of My people, and My chosen ones will wear out the work of their hands. They will not labor in vain, or bear children for calamity; for they are the offspring of those blessed by the LORD, and their descendants with them. It will also come to pass that before they call, I will answer; and while they are still speaking, I will hear."*

Nothing is impossible. I anticipate and expect because of the nature of the testimony.

> *Phil. 4:13* *"I can do all things through Him who strengthens me."*

Christ's victory is complete. I persevere and prevail because of the nature of Christ.

> *2Cor. 12:9* *"And He has said to me, 'My grace is sufficient for you, for power is perfected in weakness.' Most gladly, therefore, I will rather boast about my weaknesses, so that the power of Christ may dwell in me."*

> *Eph. 1:22-23* *"And He put all things in subjection under His feet, and gave Him as head over all things to the church, which is His body, the fullness of Him who fills all in all."*

I am significant. I walk in authority and influence because of the redeemed nature of _____ (your name).

2Cor. 3:18 *"But we all, with unveiled face, beholding as in a mirror the glory of the Lord, are being transformed into the same image from glory to glory, just as from the Lord, the Spirit."*

Col. 1:9-14 *"For this reason also, since the day we heard of it, we have not ceased to pray for you and to ask that you may be filled with the knowledge of His will in all spiritual wisdom and understanding, so that you will walk in a manner worthy of the Lord, to please Him in all respects, bearing fruit in every good work and increasing in the knowledge of God; strengthened with all power, according to His glorious might, for the attaining of all steadfastness and patience; joyously giving thanks to the Father, who has qualified us to share in the inheritance of the saints in Light. For He rescued us from the domain of darkness, and transferred us to the kingdom of His beloved Son, in whom we have redemption, the forgiveness of sins."*

Deut. 8:18 *"But you shall remember the LORD your God, for it is He who is giving you power to make wealth, that He may confirm His covenant which He swore to your fathers, as it is this day."*

John 17:20-22 *"I do not ask on behalf of these alone, but for those also who believe in Me through their word; that they may all be one; even as You, Father, are in Me and I in You, that they also may be in Us, so that the world may believe that You sent Me. The glory which You have given Me I have given to them, that they may be one, just as We are one..."*

NEW PRACTICES

I found that facing upstream required different behaviors. I began to think differently, and live in new ways. My choices and decisions were different because I changed my paradigm from lack to plenty. Understand that, apart from the occasional pleasant surprise (miracle), my circumstances had not changed. Instead, my viewpoint has changed. Using the language of Session 4, I had "tuned out" the broadcast of poverty (Ephesians 6:12) and instead tuned in to the broadcast of prosperity. I was facing upriver and I "naturally" behaved differently. My good seed was bearing fruit.

I remember walking away from the river prayer looking for good things to drift into my hands. They did. I began to recognize opportunities and favor that had passed me by before the prayer. I grabbed everything I could get my hands on.

I began to make decisions from faith. My friends noticed. My wife noticed. I noticed. I liked it and began to adopt a new way of living—believing for the best. I was climbing into the wheelbarrow with Christ.

An opportunity presented itself, a request to serve someone I admired. I enthusiastically accepted one offer, and then another. And another. Soon, I was wondering how to get it all done—my cup runneth over. I had entered the Holy Spirit School of Dominion, lesson #1.

LESSON #1

I naturally *turn* downstream. It requires an intentional act to continue to face upstream. This is because our soul, like a natural man in a natural river, will turn downstream rather than face the resistance. It is natural to face downstream, even when the river is spiritual.

There is no devil that is turning us around. Remember that the spirit of poverty—whether demon, power, or principality—is broken. If we find ourselves facing downstream now, it is because we allowed ourselves to be turned by the resistance of the current. It is "easier" to face downstream because it is not comfortable to face the "pressure" of the river. This illustration may not work fully, but my point is that each of us can intentionally face life and time. Do not hide! Do not avoid your promises!

LESSON #2

My next lesson was *rest*. When I face upstream, I encounter more opportunity than I can handle. There is so much in the river—more than I need—so this is what I did. I raced around in that river to get as much as I could. I was struggling to get everything—anything. I had not taken dominion yet because I still did not believe (TRUST) that God's river contained an inexhaustible supply of good gifts. I believed it in my mind, yet was not trusting this vital truth. I was not in the wheelbarrow. I was not resting.

In time, I am learning to say no as often as I say yes. In the river, God places things that are good, things better, and things best. I practice allowing good things to pass by. I practice allowing better things to pass by, too. And, I am learning to wait for the best, picking carefully and allowing the rest to pass on to others. I am learning generosity in the river.

By the way, I make many mistakes, even allowing the best to pass when I shouldn't. Again, God is endless, unlimited, extravagant. Guess what happened? God sent another "best." He proves Himself to be wildly faithful and gracious.

LESSON #3

I am learning that when I face upstream, I have time to position myself in the river to capture new and different gifts. In fact, He leads me to new parts of the river. Even here, He is a Wind and expects us to follow His Spirit. There is no stagnant place in Christ.

> <u>John 4:24</u> *"God is spirit, and those who worship Him must worship in spirit and truth."*

Pray with me again, looking upstream together. Close your eyes. Pray with me.

"Time (river) is flowing toward me.
There is no limitation in heaven.
God places good things in the river.
Good things flow to me.
They are easy to catch.

"I do not need to grab every thing,
because God will send me the best.
I will not settle for good or better,
only God's best for me.

"I am resting in the river.
God, teach me to see and hear.
Teach me to feel, taste, and smell.
Teach me prosperity and dominion."

Take a moment and write down anything God may speak to you now.

_____
_____
_____
_____
_____
_____
_____
_____
_____
_____

EXERCISES

Live within your means. Spend what you have left after saving, instead of saving what you have left after spending. By controlling yourself, you will practice intentional stewardship over your time and your money.

Prov. 25:28 "Like a city that is broken into and without walls is a man who has no control over his spirit."

Don't work for money, make your money work for you. Money is a willing slave, but a terrible master. How are you directing your dollars? What changes will you make? Begin to accumulate and hold one-month's payroll in a savings account. Do not spend it, only protect it. This will become your emergency fund (becoming the bank).

Put money under your dominion. Can you carry a $100 bill and not spend it? Carry it around in your wallet or checkbook and do not spend it. Do it for a week. Do it again for a month. After the month, ask God to direct your giving. When you give this $100, you will experience a new level of giving—that of the Cheerful Giver.

2Cor. 9:7 "Each one must do just as he has purposed in his heart, not grudgingly or under compulsion, for God loves a cheerful giver."

Plan a major purchase. Choose something (as a couple if you are married) or go shop for something that will last you for years (a centerpiece, a home improvement, etc.). You have to get the "more expensive version" and it cannot be purchased quickly. Instead, you must plan and save for it. It will be of the best quality available that noticeably stands out from your other things.

You will not buy it now, but you will pick it out. Go back and look at it several times. Feel free to change your mind, but change your mind before you purchase it.

Pray about it and work at it by saving money for it. Depending on the size of the item, it may take weeks or months. Once you have it, intentionally view it as a monument, a reminder. My personal example is the patio we saved for over three years. It is now a monument in our home.

List these or some other exercise you plan to try. Ask God for wisdom, and write it down here. Have fun!

_____

_____

_____

_____

_____

_____

_____

_____

_____

_____

Touch your head and say, "I am a prosperous soul."

APPENDIX ONE

Dream Worksheet

I have always dreamed about:

_____
_____
_____
_____
_____
_____
_____

I have imagined that I would:

_____
_____
_____
_____
_____
_____
_____

In the past, I have received the following prophetic words about:

_____
_____
_____
_____
_____
_____
_____

APPENDIX TWO

Working With The Fur

Once upon a time, a certain cat got saved at a Billy Graham crusade. Although this cat was born again, he struggled with vanity over his beautiful coat. The cat took great pride in his coat and asked God over and over to bless him and care for his beautiful coat. Falling asleep, the cat had a dream.

In the dream he was brought before God's majestic throne. Both God and the cat were wearing their best coats. They each admired one another's coat and gave easy compliments to each other on the character of their coats. As God reached down to pet the cat's coat, the cat backed up to God so that He could, and God began petting the cat from tail to head.

The cat awoke from the dream and pondered why God would pet the cat's coat in reverse. It obviously caused discomfort to the cat plus detracted from the elegance of his coat. Night after night, the cat continued to fall asleep and dream of God petting him from tail to head.

Greatly perplexed, the vain cat cried out to God, "Why do you insist on petting my coat from tail to head?" After some time, God gave the cat another dream. Like every dream before, God reached down to pet the cat's coat. But just as God stretched forth His hand, the cat mewed, "You made this beautiful coat, why don't you pet me like it was designed, from head to tail?"

God smiled and explained that, yes, He was the creator of that beautiful coat, but like all His creations, they are intended to serve Him and yield to His design. He had intended the coat to glorify Him, not the cat. God chose how a cat would be petted, and it was vanity that caused the cat to stand backwards. It would be the cat that was backwards, not God.

The cat awoke to understand how great and wise was his God, and understood his purpose was to honor God with his coat, not to glory in it for his own purpose. Happily, the cat repented and began serving God with his beautiful coat.

God designed our finances to lay in one direction, like the cat's fur. If we are not standing in line with God's plan, it is we who need to adjust, not God. If you are experiencing financial struggle, FIRST make sure you are not standing "AGAINST" a spiritual law.

Money is designed to serve God and man, not the other way around. Money operates under natural laws and spiritual laws. If you fight against either one, you will "pay."

APPENDIX THREE

RESOURCE LIST

BETHEL CORE VALUES

Johnson, Bill, *When Heaven Invades Earth: A Practical Guide to a Life of Miracles.* Shippensburg, PA: Destiny House, 2003. **(B)**

Johnson, Bill, *Dreaming With God.* Shippensburg, PA: Destiny House, 2006. **(B)**

Johnson, Bill, *Face to Face with God.* Shippensburg, PA: Destiny House, 2006. **(B)**

Johnson, Bill, *Strengthen Yourself in the Lord: How to Release the Hidden Power of God In Your Life.* Shippensburg, PA: Destiny House, 2007. **(B)**

Johnson, Bill, *The Supernatural Power of a Transformed Mind: Access to a Life of Miracles.* Shippensburg, PA: Destiny House, 2005. **(B)**

Vallotton, Kris with Bill Johnson, *The Supernatural Ways of Royalty.* Shippensburg, PA: Destiny House, 2006. **(B)**

Bolz, Shawn, *Keys to Heaven's Economy: An Angelic Visitation from the Minister of Finance.* North Sutton, NH: Streams Publishing House, 2005. **(B)**

DeSilva, Stephen K., *Wealth Factor.* Redding, CA: Bethel Church, 2007. **(A)**

FINANCIAL BASICS

Kiyosaki, Robert T., *Rich Dad, Poor Dad: What the Rich Teach Their Kids About Money—That the Poor and Middle Class Do Not!* New York, NY: Warner Books, 1997 **(B)**

Kiyosaki, Robert T., *Rich Dad's Prophecy: Why the Biggest Stock Market Crash in History Is Still Coming…and How You Can Prepare Yourself and Profit from It!* New York, NY: Warner Books, 2002. **(B)**

Clason, George S., *The Richest Man in Babylon.* New York, NY: Penguin Putnam, 1988. **(B)**

DeSilva, Stephen K., *Prosperous Soul Stewardship Series: Keys For New Couples.* Redding, CA: Bethel Church, 2007. **(V)**

OVERCOMING POVERTY

DeSilva, Stephen K., *Prosperous Soul Stewardship Series: Foundations.* Redding, CA: Bethel Church, 2007. **(A)**

Johnson, Bill, *Breaking the Spirit of Poverty.* Redding, CA: Bethel Church, 1996. **(A)**

Vallotton, Kris, *From Paupers to Princes.* Redding, CA: Bethel Church, 2002. **(A)**

Eberle, Harold R., *Developing a Prosperous Soul Volume 1: How to Overcome a Poverty Mind-set.* Yakima, WA: Winepress, 1997. **(B)**

Eberle, Harold R., *Developing a Prosperous Soul Volume 2: How to Move Into God's Financial Blessings.* Yakima, WA: Winepress, 1997. **(B)**

LEADERSHIP & BUSINESS

Gerber, Michael E., *The E-Myth Revisited: Why Most Small Businesses Don't Work and What to Do About It.* New York, NY: HarperCollins, 1995. **(B)**

Kiyosaki, Robert T. and Sharon L. Lechter, *Cash Flow Quadrant: Rich Dad's Guide to Financial Freedom.* New York, NY: Warner Books, 1998. **(B)**

Covey, Stephen R., *The 7 Habits of Highly Effective People.* New York, NY: Free Press, 1989, 2004. **(B)**

Maxwell, John C., *Developing the Leader Within You.* Nashville, TN: Thomas Nelson, 1993. **(B)**

ADVANCED READING FOR ENTREPRENEURS

Collins, Jim, *Good to Great: Why Some Companies Make the Leap...and Others Don't.* New York, NY: HarperCollins, 2001. **B)**

Pink, Daniel H., *A Whole New Mind: Why Right-Brainers Will Rule the Future.* New York, NY: Penguin Group, 2005. **(B)**

Taleb, Nassim Nichol, *The Black Swan: The Impact of the Highly Improbable.* New York, NY: Random House, 2007. **(B)**

Gerber, Michael E., *E-Myth Mastery: The Seven Essential Disciplines for Building a World Class Company.* New York, NY: HarperCollins, 2005. **(B)**

Sachs, Jeffrey D., *The End of Poverty: Economic Possibilities for Our Time.* New York, NY: Penguin Group, 2005. **(B)**

Stanley, Thomas J. Ph.D., *The Millionaire Mind.* Kansas City, MO: Andrews McMeel, 2001. **(B)**

B=Book A=Audio V=Video

APPENDIX FOUR

Bethel Church Offering Declarations

In 2001, Bill Johnson was impressed enough by an offering declaration at another church body that he decided to obtain a copy of the words for his Bethel Church family. Since that first Sunday, the offering declaration has become a common fixture of our weekly services. As a church body, we alternate between these two readings, holding our gifts before us, declaring as unto the Lord the purpose of our offering.

OFFERING DECLARATION #1

As we receive today's offering
We are believing the Lord for:

Jobs and better jobs, raises and bonuses
Benefits, sales and commissions
Favorable settlements, estates and inheritances
Interests and income, rebates and returns
Checks in the mail, gifts and surprises
Finding money, debts paid off
Expenses decrease, blessing and increase.

Thank you Lord
For meeting all of my financial needs
That I may have more than enough
To give into the Kingdom of God
And promote the Gospel of Jesus Christ

Hallelujah!

OFFERING DECLARATION #2

As we receive today's offering
we are believing You for

Heaven open, earth invaded
Storehouses unlocked, and miracles created

Dreams and visions, angelic visitations
Declarations, visitations, and divine manifestations

Anointing, gifting and calls, positions and promotions,
Provisions and resources, to go to the nations

Souls and more souls, from every generation,
Saved and set free, carrying Kingdom revelation!

Thank you, Father,
that as I join my value system to Yours,
You will shower favor, blessings and increase upon me
so I have more than enough
to co-labor with heaven
to see Jesus get his full reward!

Hallelujah!

END NOTES

Unless otherwise indicated, all Scripture quotations are taken from the New American Standard Bible.

INTRODUCTION

[1]3John 1:2 Beloved, I pray that in all respects you may prosper and be in good health, just as your soul prospers.

[2]Matthew 6:10 Your kingdom come. Your will be done, on earth as it is in heaven.

[3]Genesis chapters 37 through 50.

[4]Luke 19:16-17 The first appeared, saying, "Master, your mina has made ten minas more." And he said to him, "Well done, good slave, because you have been faithful in a very little thing, you are to be in authority over ten cities."

[5]Col. 1:9 For this reason also, since the day we heard of it, we have not ceased to pray for you and to ask that you may be filled with the knowledge of His will in all spiritual wisdom and understanding.

SESSION 1

[1]SOZO is a Greek word meaning *to save*. It is translated as *bring safely, cured, get well, insure salvation, made well, preserved, recover, restore, save, saved, saves,* and *saving*. It is used in connection with salvation in Luke 19:10 and

Romans 10:9, healing in Matthew 9:22, and deliverance in Luke 8:36 and Romans 11:26. Here, I use this word in the context of prayer that saves, heals, and delivers a person from some unbiblical and deeply-held belief. See also John 3:17, Ephesians 2:8, and Titus 3:5. For further information on the SOZO ministry, call Bethel Church Transformation Center (530.246.6000) or look online at www.ibethel.org/churchlife/sozo.

[2]Psalm 91

[3]Matthew 6:12-15 And forgive us our debts, as we also have forgiven our debtors. And do not lead us into temptation, but deliver us from evil. For Yours is the kingdom and the power and the glory forever. Amen. For if you forgive others for their transgressions, your heavenly Father will also forgive you. But if you do not forgive others, then your Father will not forgive your transgressions.

SESSION 2

[1]Matt. 1:23 Behold, the virgin shall be with child and shall bear a son, and they shall call his name "Immanuel," which translated means, "God with us."

[2]John 1:50 Jesus answered and said to him, "Because I said to you that I saw you under the fig tree, do you believe? You will see greater things than these."

[3]Taleb, Nassim. (2007). *The Black Swan: The Impact of the Highly Improbable.* New York: Random House. Page xvii.

[4]Rev. 19:10 Then I fell at his feet to worship him. But he said to me, "Do not do that; I am a fellow servant of yours and your brethren who hold the testimony of Jesus; worship God. For the testimony of Jesus is the spirit of prophecy."

[5]Jorgensen, Owen. (1994). *Supernatural: The Life of William Branham, Book Three: The Man and His Commission (1946-1950).* Tucson, AZ: Tucson Tabernacle. Page 46.

[6]Prov. 18:21 Death and life are in the power of the tongue, and those who love it will eat its fruit.

[7]Matt. 12:34 You brood of vipers, how can you, being evil, speak what is good? For the mouth speaks out of that which fills the heart.

[8]1Cor. 13:13 But now faith, hope, love, abide these three; but the greatest of these is love.

[9]2Cor. 3:18 But we all, with unveiled face, beholding as in a mirror the glory of the Lord, are being transformed into the same image from glory to glory, just as from the Lord, the Spirit.

[10]Sachs, Jeffrey. (2005). *The End of Poverty: Economic Possibilities for Our Time.* New York: Penguin Books. Page 1.

[11]Sachs, Jeffrey. (2005). *The End of Poverty: Economic Possibilities for Our Time.* New York: Penguin Books. Pages 18-19.

SESSION 3

[1]Mal. 3:7-12 "From the days of your fathers you have turned aside from My statutes and have not kept them. Return to Me, and I will return to you," says the LORD of hosts. "But you say, 'How shall we return?' Will a man rob God? Yet you are robbing Me! But you say, 'How have we robbed You?' In tithes and offerings. You are cursed with a curse, for you are robbing Me, the whole nation of you! Bring the whole tithe into the storehouse, so that there may be food in My house, and test Me now in this," says the LORD of hosts, "if I will not open for you the windows of heaven and pour out for you a blessing until it overflows. Then I will rebuke the devourer for you, so that it will not destroy the fruits of the ground; nor will your vine in the field cast its grapes," says the LORD of hosts. "All the nations will call you blessed, for you shall be a delightful land," says the LORD of hosts.

[2]John 15:1-11 I am the true vine, and My Father is the vinedresser. Every branch in Me that does not bear fruit, He takes away; and every branch that bears fruit, He prunes it so that it may bear more fruit. You are already clean because of the word which I have spoken to you. Abide in Me, and I in you. As the branch cannot bear fruit of itself unless it abides in the vine, so neither can you unless you abide in Me. I am the vine, you are the branches; he who abides in Me and I in him, he bears much fruit, for apart from Me you can do nothing. If anyone does not abide in Me, he is thrown away as a branch and dries up; and they gather them, and cast them into the fire and they are burned. If you abide in Me, and My words abide in you, ask whatever you wish, and it will be done for you. My Father is glorified by this, that you bear much fruit, and so prove to be My disciples. Just as the Father has loved Me, I have also loved you; abide in My love. If you keep My commandments, you will abide in My love; just as I have kept My Father's commandments and abide in His love. These things I have spoken to you so that My joy may be in you, and that your joy may be made full.

[3]Prov. 14:23 In all labor there is profit, but mere talk leads only to poverty.

SESSION 4

[1]Tim. 1:4 nor to pay attention to myths and endless genealogies, which give rise to mere speculation rather than furthering the administration of God which is by faith.

[2]Frangipane, Francis. (1989). *The Three Battlegrounds*. Cedar Rapids, Indiana: Arrow Publications. Page 133.

[3]Covey, Stephen. (1989). *The 7 Habits of Highly Effective People*. New York: Free Press. Pages 23-31.

SESSION 5

[1]Hag. 2:7 "And I will shake all nations, and the desire of all nations shall come: and I will fill this house with glory," saith the LORD of hosts. (KJV)

[2]*Leadership Advance Audio CD. Session 5: Pastor Bill Johnson.* Tuesday, May 8, 2007. 7:00pm.

SESSION 6

[1]I captured these notes from a staff meeting in 2007. During those meetings, various pastors share their heart on many issues. One day, Bill Johnson began to discuss an idea he had of foundational structures of heaven. He called those pillars the *Four Pillars of Heaven.* I captured those ideas and comments and presented them here for your prayerful consideration.